Surah Al-Hujurat

Surah Al-Hujurat Workbook
e ISBN 978-967-2844-13-6

First Edition: December 2021

Authors and Editors:
Maria Marzuki, Kritika Sharifuddin, Faridah Idris, Putri Shahnim Khalid

✉ workbookquran@gmail.com
 Qur'an Workbook for all
 @quranworkbook

Typesetting & Illustration: Inda Hayati Samsi
Cover Design: Inda Hayati Samsi

Printed in Malaysia.

Charity Reg. No. 1143245

www.karimia.com
Email: **info@karimia.com**

Re: Permission to use the Majestic Quran translation and headings

I received the first workbook on Surah Al Kahfi early 2020. I was pleased to see the workbook used section headings from my Quran translation. The authors have put a lot of effort to make the workbook useful for Quran learners.

I am pleased that the new Quran workbook series have been published fully using the Majestic Quran translation and section headings. I have reviewed all three workbooks for Surah Al-Mulk, Surah Al-Hujurat and Surah As-Sajdah.

These are excellent workbooks. The colour scheme and the Arabic is attractive. The reflection questions are thought provoking for those who need guidance on doing tadabbur of the surahs. Furthermore, the workbooks conform with teachings of Islam and invite people to Quran in an inspiring and entertaining manner. So I give them permission to cite the Majestic Quran's translation and headings.

May Allah bless this effort, the authors and all those who assist in the making of these workbooks to completion.

Wassalam

Dr. Musharraf Hussain OBE, DL

CEO and Chief Imam Karimia institute

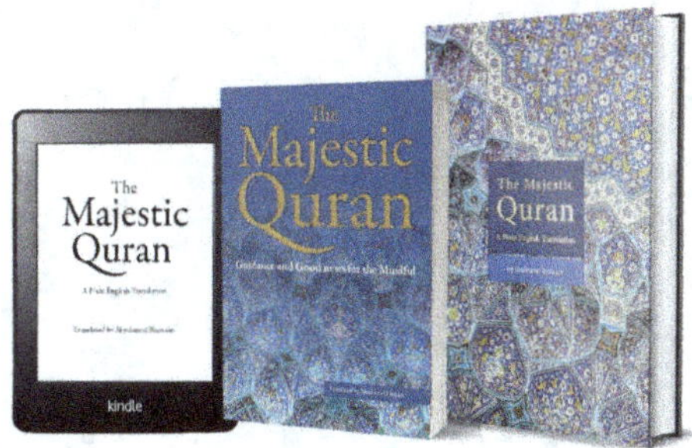

www.**majesticquran**.co.uk

Bobbers mill Community centre 512-514 Berridge Road west, Hyson Green, Nottingham NG7 5JU
Tel. 0115 8415806

TABLE OF CONTENT

INTRODUCTION

Alhamdulillah thumma Alhamdulillah,

by the grace of Allah, our second Qur'an Workbook is published after Covid-19 "MCO" (movement control order) was lifted in October 2021. Just when we think that being confined at home means more time, Allah ﷻ is always the best of planners. Everything has its time and we are always where we are meant to be. We pray to Allah Al-Syaafii that when this workbook reaches you, you are in the best state of eeman and health. For the users of Al-Kahf workbook, we pray that you have had a meaningful tadabbur journey and that the workbook serves its purpose for your learning. Thank you for following our social media and telegram channel. Forgive our shortcomings if your queries are not responded instantly.

If you had read "Our Story" from the first workbook, Al-Kahf, you would know that we design this workbook from the perspective of a learner. A few years later, we are still students of the Qur'an. We are still reflecting upon His signs and His words. We are still pondering over the essence and the depth of the message of this divine book. How can we not? The Qur'an is our companion for life.

The second publication of Qur'an workbook is not one but three surahs - Al-Mulk, As-Sajdah and Al-Hujurat. Reason being, the first two are the two surahs that our Prophet ﷺ recites every night before sleep[1]. Hence we should engage deeper with Al-Mulk and As-Sajdah, and appreciate how they would benefit us.

[1] *It was narrated from Jaabir, that the Prophet ﷺ never used to sleep until he had recited Alif-laam-meem tanzeel [al-Sajdah] and Tabaarak alladhi bi yadihi'l-mulk [al-Mulk].*

Narrated by al-Tirmidhi, 2892; Al-Albaani said in Saheeh al-Tirmidhi(3/6) that this hadeeth is saheeh.

As for the latter, we believe that next to Al-Kahf, Al-Hujurat also speaks of another aspect of trial faced by the ummah - ethics and moral values. We hope to invite every Muslim to reflect further upon this surah where Allah ﷻ calls upon the believers specifically, through *Ya ayyuha alladhina aamanu*, 5 times!

The purpose of this workbook remains the same. **If you are a beginner, we want this to be the entry point for your interaction and relationship with the Qur'an. If you are already students of the Qur'an, regardless of your progress, we hope this workbook will facilitate you to a more meaningful and deeper relationship with the Words of Allah.**

We have decided to continue using *The Majestic Qur'an, a Plain English Translation by Dr Musharraf* Hussain for the sections of the surah and also his translation for this workbook. We have included a comprehensive list of references and suggestions for further reading and study. If you need more space to ink your thoughts and reflection, the blank templates are downloadable. You may refer to our Facebook page for further details.

Have a blessed journey, friends. Let us take a moment to renew our intentions, for intentions are dynamic and challenging to perfect. We aim for the barakah in this life and the next, and may Allah make the Qur'an the spring of our hearts and the means to attain that barakah we seek and need. الله يبارك فيكم.

Your sisters in Islam,

Maria Marzuki
Kritika Sharifuddin
Faridah Idris
Putri Shahnim Khalid

November 2021
Malaysia.

✉ quranworkbook@gmail.com
◻ Qur'an Workbook for all
◻ @quranworkbook
◻ @quranworkbook

HOW TO USE THIS WORKBOOK

This workbook consists of several components :

Overview of the surah

This provides the general information of the surah. Qur'an learners are encouraged to find the answers for this section on their own.

Sections of the surah

The surah is divided into different sections with the title representing the section's content. In each section, we have the Arabic verses and the English translation. Few selected words or verses are highlighted in the section for the students to pay close attention to and further explore the significance of the word(s).

Reflection page

Each section is followed by a reflection page. A question and a gem statement are provided to initiate your reflection process. The subsequent two empty pages are there for you to populate your thoughts with lessons learnt and action plans.

Allah's Names and Attributes

This is a new section for Qur'an learners to reflect on the beautiful Names and Attributes of Allah that come in the surah and where they are positioned.

Appendix

The appendix is meant for you to refer to additional materials and resources that will make your Qur'an journey richer and more meaningful.

Disclaimer: the information in this workbook is meant to supplement your Qur'an studies in conjunction with onsite and online classes/lectures, not to be used solely on its own.

Note : This is only a suggestion. You may have your own way to do reflection and you are free to use any approach that works best for you.

1. Purify your intention and make du'a to ease your journey and protection from Shaytan.

2. Understand your learning goals. You can design your own learning plan to ensure consistency and continuity of learning.

3. Choose one learning platform/classes/materials to get you started with this study. You can refer to the list of references and resources.

4. Read the overview of the surah, learn what it is all about.

5. Recite the verses of the section you are studying. Remember there is barakah in recitation.

6. Read the translation given or use your preferred translation. You may want to study the tafseer or listen to any lecture to get a deeper understanding.

7. You can write the word-to-word translation under each Arabic word in the section.

8. Start your reflection by using the question and gem given in the reflection page to help you reflect on the verses and the section.

9. Pay extra attention to the highlighted words or verse in the section. Try to find the connection between the words and the section.

10. Ink down anything that comes to mind in the empty spaces given. Be creative!

11. Document the lessons learnt and your plan in the subsequent empty pages. Do not worry about getting too structured. Your points may overlap and that is perfectly okay.

12. You can refer to the appendix to get more reflection questions for each section to further facilitate your reflection process.

13. Refer to your local Qur'an scholar or teacher if you have any questions or doubts about the verse.

14. You can do this on your own or you can do it in a group and share your reflection with each other.

15. Do not let a moment of difficulty hinders you from moving forward. What matters is progress, not perfection.

May Allah ease and bless our effort to sincerely understand and reflect on His Words. اللَّهُمَّ اَمِين

REFLECTION TIPS

Recite. Reflect. Implement.

"Reflection is the lamp of the heart; if it departs the heart will have no light."
-Ibn Ata'illah (Hikam)

Pondering and reflection requires deep thought process and time for the process to bear fruit. And sometimes, you need to visualise the verses and relate to our current time. Most importantly, it is to see the verses through the lens of our eyes with the intention to reform our own hearts and self. So here are some steps and questions that can help your reflection process.

Steps to do reflection

1. Read the verse in Arabic and then read the translation. Consider reading multiple translations to get different perspectives.

2. Read the tafseer of the verse to get some background information on the verse to facilitate the process.

3. Take note of the things that capture your attention.

4. Develop action points or practical steps from your reading of the verse.

Questions to facilitate the reflection process

1. What comes to mind when you read the verse?

2. What is the main message of this verse?

3. What reminder do you get from reading the verse?

4. What have you learned from this verse?

5. How can you apply the lessons and reminders in different facets of your life?

Reflection process leads to implementation of action goals or points that you derive from the process. May Allah open up your mind to the depth of the reflection process and make you act upon the Qur'an. اللهم امين

سُبْحَـٰنَكَ لَا عِلْمَ لَنَآ إِلَّا مَا عَلَّمْتَنَآ إِنَّكَ أَنتَ ٱلْعَلِيمُ ٱلْحَكِيمُ

Exalted are You; we have absolutely no knowledge except what You have taught us. Indeed, it is You who is the Knowing, the Wise. [2:32]

Revelation: Qur'anic Year ☐ of 23 — Makki / Madani surah
Sequence in mushaf: ☐ of 114 surah
Total of ☐ verses

Get to know Surah Al-Hujurat

https://bit.ly/overviewAlHujurat

MANNERS OF MEETING AND GREETING THE MESSENGER

بِسْمِ اللَّهِ الرَّحْمَٰنِ الرَّحِيمِ

يَٰٓأَيُّهَا ٱلَّذِينَ ءَامَنُوا۟ لَا تُقَدِّمُوا۟ بَيْنَ يَدَىِ ٱللَّهِ وَرَسُولِهِۦ ۖ وَٱتَّقُوا۟ ٱللَّهَ ۚ إِنَّ ٱللَّهَ سَمِيعٌ عَلِيمٌ ﴿١﴾

يَٰٓأَيُّهَا ٱلَّذِينَ ءَامَنُوا۟ لَا تَرْفَعُوٓا۟ أَصْوَٰتَكُمْ فَوْقَ صَوْتِ ٱلنَّبِىِّ وَلَا تَجْهَرُوا۟ لَهُۥ بِٱلْقَوْلِ كَجَهْرِ بَعْضِكُمْ

لِبَعْضٍ أَن تَحْبَطَ أَعْمَٰلُكُمْ وَأَنتُمْ لَا تَشْعُرُونَ ﴿٢﴾ إِنَّ ٱلَّذِينَ يَغُضُّونَ أَصْوَٰتَهُمْ عِندَ رَسُولِ ٱللَّهِ

أُو۟لَٰٓئِكَ ٱلَّذِينَ ٱمْتَحَنَ ٱللَّهُ قُلُوبَهُمْ لِلتَّقْوَىٰ ۚ لَهُم مَّغْفِرَةٌ وَأَجْرٌ عَظِيمٌ ﴿٣﴾

إِنَّ ٱلَّذِينَ يُنَادُونَكَ مِن وَرَآءِ ٱلْحُجُرَٰتِ أَكْثَرُهُمْ لَا يَعْقِلُونَ ﴿٤﴾

وَلَوْ أَنَّهُمْ صَبَرُوا۟ حَتَّىٰ تَخْرُجَ إِلَيْهِمْ لَكَانَ خَيْرًا لَّهُمْ ۚ وَٱللَّهُ غَفُورٌ رَّحِيمٌ ﴿٥﴾

[1] **Believers! Do not put yourselves ahead of** Allah and His Messenger; be fearful of Allah. Indeed, Allah is the Hearer, the Knower. [2] **Believers, don't raise your voices** above the voice of the Prophet, nor talk loudly with him as you might talk loudly with each other, your deeds will be ruined without you knowing. [3] Those who lower their voices in the presence of the Messenger of Allah are the ones whose hearts Allah has selected for piety. Forgiveness and a great reward awaits them. [4] Most of those who called out to you from outside your home don't understand. [5] It would have been **far better** for them had they **waited patiently** till you came out. Allah is Forgiving, Caring.

When Allah calls upon the believers specifically in the Qur'an, how does the call affect your heart?

Qur'anic Gem

Patience brings calmness in our conduct and that leads to beautiful manners.

What can I do better for the sake of Allah?

WHEN YOU HEAR NEWS, CHECK THE FACTS

يَا أَيُّهَا الَّذِينَ آمَنُوٓا إِن جَاءَكُمْ فَاسِقٌ بِنَبَإٍ فَتَبَيَّنُوٓا أَن تُصِيبُوا قَوْمًا بِجَهَالَةٍ

فَتُصْبِحُوا عَلَىٰ مَا فَعَلْتُمْ نَادِمِينَ ﴿٦﴾

وَٱعْلَمُوٓا أَنَّ فِيكُمْ رَسُولَ ٱللَّهِ ۚ لَوْ يُطِيعُكُمْ فِي كَثِيرٍ مِّنَ ٱلْأَمْرِ

لَعَنِتُّمْ وَلَٰكِنَّ ٱللَّهَ حَبَّبَ إِلَيْكُمُ ٱلْإِيمَانَ وَزَيَّنَهُ فِي قُلُوبِكُمْ

وَكَرَّهَ إِلَيْكُمُ ٱلْكُفْرَ وَٱلْفُسُوقَ وَٱلْعِصْيَانَ ۚ أُو۟لَٰٓئِكَ هُمُ ٱلرَّاشِدُونَ ﴿٧﴾

فَضْلًا مِّنَ ٱللَّهِ وَنِعْمَةً ۚ وَٱللَّهُ عَلِيمٌ حَكِيمٌ ﴿٨﴾

⁶ **Believers,** if a discredited person brings you news, then **check** *it* in case you cause harm to others ignorantly, and then later regret what you did. ⁷ Remember, the Messenger of Allah is among you. If he frequently followed your wishes then you would suffer *badly*; however, Allah has made faith beloved and highly attractive for you hearts, and made disbelief, sin and disobedience dislikeable to you. **These are the rightly guided,** ⁸ *given* grace as a gift from Allah, the Knower, Wise.

This is the third call to all believers, followed by a command to verify news. Are you amongst those who spread news before verifying? Who then, are the 'Rashidoon'?

What can I do better for the sake of Allah?

وَإِن طَآئِفَتَانِ مِنَ ٱلْمُؤْمِنِينَ ٱقْتَتَلُوا۟ فَأَصْلِحُوا۟ بَيْنَهُمَا

فَإِنۢ بَغَتْ إِحْدَىٰهُمَا عَلَى ٱلْأُخْرَىٰ فَقَٰتِلُوا۟ ٱلَّتِى تَبْغِى حَتَّىٰ تَفِىٓءَ إِلَىٰٓ أَمْرِ ٱللَّهِ

فَإِن فَآءَتْ فَأَصْلِحُوا۟ بَيْنَهُمَا بِٱلْعَدْلِ وَأَقْسِطُوٓا۟ إِنَّ ٱللَّهَ يُحِبُّ ٱلْمُقْسِطِينَ ۞

إِنَّمَا ٱلْمُؤْمِنُونَ إِخْوَةٌ فَأَصْلِحُوا۟ بَيْنَ أَخَوَيْكُمْ وَٱتَّقُوا۟ ٱللَّهَ لَعَلَّكُمْ تُرْحَمُونَ ۞

⁹ If two groups of believers fight, then you must **make peace** between them. If one of them is unjust to the other, then fight the unjust until he accepts Allah's judgement. If he accepts it then make peace between them fairly, and be just. **Indeed, Allah loves the just.** ¹⁰ The believers are brothers, so make peace between two brothers; be mindful of Allah so you might be cared for.

Did you know that to make peace between believers is a command, not merely a culture? Why is justice essential to society?

Qur'anic Gem

Islam promotes peace and justice. One cannot exist without the other.

What can I do better for the sake of Allah?

BEHAVIOURS THAT LEAD TO CONFLICT

يَـٰٓأَيُّهَا ٱلَّذِينَ ءَامَنُواْ لَا يَسْخَرْ قَوْمٌ مِّن قَوْمٍ عَسَىٰٓ أَن يَكُونُواْ خَيْرًا مِّنْهُمْ

وَلَا نِسَآءٌ مِّن نِّسَآءٍ عَسَىٰٓ أَن يَكُنَّ خَيْرًا مِّنْهُنَّ

وَلَا تَلْمِزُوٓاْ أَنفُسَكُمْ وَلَا تَنَابَزُواْ بِٱلْأَلْقَـٰبِ بِئْسَ ٱلِٱسْمُ ٱلْفُسُوقُ بَعْدَ ٱلْإِيمَـٰنِ

وَمَن لَّمْ يَتُبْ فَأُوْلَـٰٓئِكَ هُمُ ٱلظَّـٰلِمُونَ ﴿١١﴾

[11] **Believers! Let no man make fun of another**, he might be better than him; **no woman should make fun of other women**, they may be better than them; **nor speak ill, nor use offensive nicknames** for one another. How bad it is to be called "a trouble maker," after accepting faith. Those who don't turn away from such behaviour are wicked.

This is the fourth call to all believers, followed by prohibitions to not ridicule, to not defame and to not offense one another with bad nicknames. Think about each and how they are different or similar. Why did Allah go out of his way to mention the men and women separately?

Qur'anic Gem

Issues come and go. Before getting ourselves involved in it, think on how is this going to affect my akhirah.

Ustaz Syaari Ab Rahman

What can I do better for the sake of Allah?

يَٰٓأَيُّهَا ٱلَّذِينَ ءَامَنُواْ ٱجْتَنِبُواْ كَثِيرًا مِّنَ ٱلظَّنِّ إِنَّ بَعْضَ ٱلظَّنِّ إِثْمٌ

وَلَا تَجَسَّسُواْ وَلَا يَغْتَب بَّعْضُكُم بَعْضًا

أَيُحِبُّ أَحَدُكُمْ أَن يَأْكُلَ لَحْمَ أَخِيهِ مَيْتًا فَكَرِهْتُمُوهُ

وَٱتَّقُواْ ٱللَّهَ إِنَّ ٱللَّهَ تَوَّابٌ رَّحِيمٌ ۝

This is the fifth and last call to all believers, followed by 3 more prohibitions. Reflect upon each and how evil they are. How is suspicion, sinful?

Qur'anic Gem

Respect must be earned. Mutual respect is lived!

What can I do better for the sake of Allah?

يَٰٓأَيُّهَا ٱلنَّاسُ

إِنَّا خَلَقْنَٰكُم مِّن ذَكَرٍ وَأُنثَىٰ وَجَعَلْنَٰكُمْ شُعُوبًا وَقَبَآئِلَ لِتَعَارَفُوٓا۟

إِنَّ أَكْرَمَكُمْ عِندَ ٱللَّهِ أَتْقَىٰكُمْ

إِنَّ ٱللَّهَ عَلِيمٌ خَبِيرٌ ﴿١٣﴾

[13] **People**! We created you from a male and a female, *then* made you into different races and tribes **so you may know each other**. Indeed, the most honourable in the sight of Allah is the most mindful of Allah, the Knower, the Aware.

After 5 specific calls to the believers, Allah calls out to all mankind of all religions and races. What is His one command to the human race? Who is said to be most noble in Allah's sight?

Qur'anic Gem

Stop pleasing people and start pleasing Allah.

What can I do better for the sake of Allah?

۞ قَالَتِ ٱلْأَعْرَابُ ءَامَنَّا ۖ قُل لَّمْ تُؤْمِنُوا۟ وَلَٰكِن قُولُوٓا۟ أَسْلَمْنَا وَلَمَّا يَدْخُلِ ٱلْإِيمَٰنُ فِى قُلُوبِكُمْ ۖ

وَإِن تُطِيعُوا۟ ٱللَّهَ وَرَسُولَهُۥ لَا يَلِتْكُم مِّنْ أَعْمَٰلِكُمْ شَيْـًٔا ۚ إِنَّ ٱللَّهَ غَفُورٌ رَّحِيمٌ ۝

إِنَّمَا ٱلْمُؤْمِنُونَ ٱلَّذِينَ ءَامَنُوا۟ بِٱللَّهِ وَرَسُولِهِۦ ثُمَّ لَمْ يَرْتَابُوا۟ وَجَٰهَدُوا۟ بِأَمْوَٰلِهِمْ وَأَنفُسِهِمْ فِى سَبِيلِ ٱللَّهِ ۚ

أُو۟لَٰٓئِكَ هُمُ ٱلصَّٰدِقُونَ ۝ قُلْ أَتُعَلِّمُونَ ٱللَّهَ بِدِينِكُمْ وَٱللَّهُ يَعْلَمُ

مَا فِى ٱلسَّمَٰوَٰتِ وَمَا فِى ٱلْأَرْضِ ۚ وَٱللَّهُ بِكُلِّ شَىْءٍ عَلِيمٌ ۝

يَمُنُّونَ عَلَيْكَ أَنْ أَسْلَمُوا۟ ۖ قُل لَّا تَمُنُّوا۟ عَلَىَّ إِسْلَٰمَكُم ۖ

بَلِ ٱللَّهُ يَمُنُّ عَلَيْكُمْ أَنْ هَدَىٰكُمْ لِلْإِيمَٰنِ إِن كُنتُمْ صَٰدِقِينَ ۝

إِنَّ ٱللَّهَ يَعْلَمُ غَيْبَ ٱلسَّمَٰوَٰتِ وَٱلْأَرْضِ ۚ وَٱللَّهُ بَصِيرٌۢ بِمَا تَعْمَلُونَ ۝

14 The Bedouins say, "We believe," tell them: "You haven't believed yet, you should say, 'We have submitted.' Faith hasn't fully entered their hearts. Had they obeyed Allah and His Messenger, none of their deeds would be lost. Indeed, Allah is Forgiving, the Caring. 15 True believers are those who believed in Allah and His Messenger, and have no doubts. They strive with their wealth and their lives in Allah's way. **They are the truthful.** 16 Are you teaching Allah your religion? Allah knows what is in the Heavens and the Earth; Allah knows all things. 17 They think they have done you a favour by embracing Islam; say: "By embracing Islam, you haven't done me any favour; *in fact* Allah has done you a favour. He has guided you to the faith, **if you are true in faith.** 18 Allah knows the secrets of Heaven and the Earth, and Allah sees all you do."

**What are the signs that faith has truly entered our hearts?
What does it even mean?**

What can I do better for the sake of Allah?

REFLECTION ON ALLAH'S NAMES & ATTRIBUTES

1. As-Samee Al-'Aleem

In Ayah 1, Allah pairs these two attributes. Reflect upon each name individually and the wisdom of them together. These names and attributes appear together around 30 times in the Qur'an.

Allah hears and is aware of all secrets without exception. He hears everything people say and whatever His creation utters. Nothing is hidden from Him, and He is the All-Hearing who answers the prayer of those who pray to Him

He is the One whose knowledge is comprehensive and extends to everything seen and unseen, apparent and hidden. Nothing whatsoever is hidden from Him and He knows what was in the past, what is in the present, and will be in the future.

2. **Al-Ghafur Ar-Raheem**

In Ayah 5, Allah pairs these two names & attributes. Reflect upon each individually and the wisdom of them together. They appear nearly 50 times together in the Qur'an

He is the One who forgives sins and accepts the repentance of all those who turn to Him; He conceals the sins of His servants, shows never-ending compassion to them and lavishes kindness on them.

Allah's comprehensive mercy which He shows to all His creation without exception by creating them and providing for them, and the particular mercy that He has exclusively for the believers, both in this life and in the hereafter.

3. **Al-'Aleem Al-Hakeem**

In Ayah 8, Allah pairs these two names. Reflect upon each name individually and the wisdom of them together. They appear over 20 times together in the Qur'an. In this surah, Allah repeats the fact that He is All-Knowing of everything in ayah 16.

He is the One whose knowledge is comprehensive and extends to everything seen and unseen, apparent and hidden. Nothing whatsoever is hidden from Him and He knows what was in the past, what is in the present, and will be in the future.

He has supreme wisdom in everything, in whatever He has decreed, in His legislation and reward and punishment on the Day of Judgement. He has given everything its perfect form and created everything in the best possible manner. He never creates anything in vain, nor does He legislate or judge in vain. He does things in His absolute wisdom.

4. At-Tawwaab Ar-Raheem

In Ayah 12, Allah pairs these two attributes. Reflect upon each name individually and the wisdom of them together. They are paired in Surah Al-Baqarah and Surah at-Tawbah as well.

He is the One who helps His slaves repent and submit completely to Him after turning to Him, and then He accepts their repentance and pardons their sins.

Allah's comprehensive mercy which He shows to all His creation without exception by creating them and providing for them, and the particular mercy that He has exclusively for the believers, both in this life and in the hereafter.

5. Al-'Aleem Al-Khabeer

In Ayah 13, Allah pairs these two attributes. Reflect upon each name individually and the wisdom of them together. They are paired in Surah Luqman and Surah at-Tahreem as well.

He is the One whose knowledge is comprehensive and extends to everything seen and unseen, apparent and hidden. Nothing whatsoever is hidden from Him and He knows what was in the past, what is in the present, and will be in the future.

He is fully aware of everything: apparent, hidden, all the secrets, and what is yet more hidden.

6. **Al-Baseer**

This surah ends with Allah telling us, He is Baseer upon everything that we do. Reflect upon this name and how it makes a powerful ending to every single message sent to us in this surah.

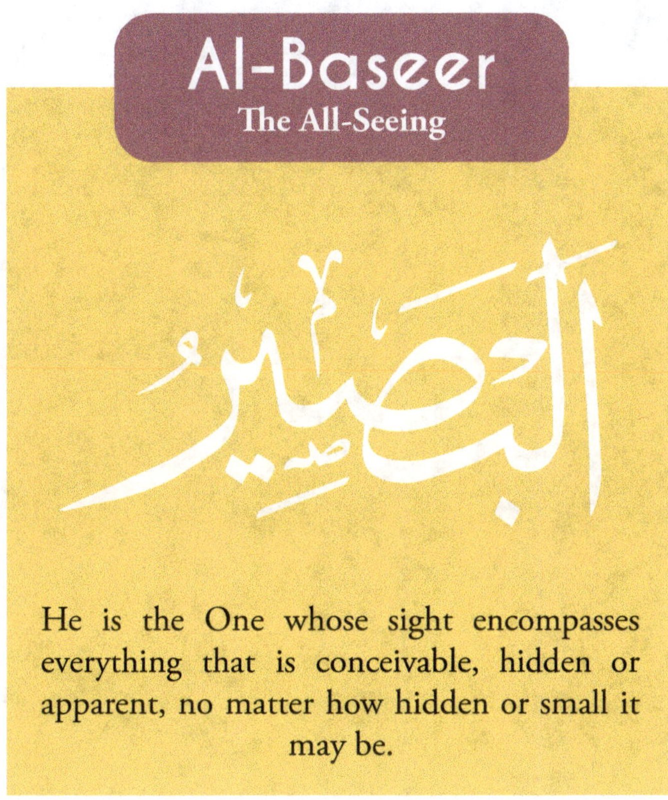

HEART THERAPY WITH DU'A

Manners and behaviours are reflections of our inner selves. With all the problems we are facing in this century, we cannot hope to overcome them without looking at their root causes: the state of our hearts. We cannot face the troubles of this world alone. We need hearts that are willing to listen to Allah and follow His guidance. Then only we will gain the strength and wisdom to solve what seems unsolvable.

Refer to Qur'an Surah Al-A'raf ayah 146. The flawed hearts perpetuate disagreements, dissension and infighting. Purifying our hearts will bring us closer to unity and love that the earliest generations enjoyed.

In a hadith narration, Abu Huraira reported: The Prophet, peace and blessings be upon him, said:

يَدْخُلُ الْجَنَّةَ أَقْوَامٌ أَفْئِدَتُهُمْ مِثْلُ أَفْئِدَةِ الطَّيْرِ

People whose hearts are like the hearts of birds will enter Paradise.
Source: Sahih Muslim 2840, Grade: Sahih (https://sunnah.com/muslim:2840)

Al-Nawawi commented on this tradition, writing:

قيل معْنَاهُ مُتَوَكِّلُون وقيلَ قُلُوبُهُمْ رقيقةٌ

It is interpreted to mean they are those who rely upon Allah, or those who have soft hearts.
Source: Riyad al-Salihin 1/45

Let us check our hearts, purify our hearts by making du'a. Be the change we want to see in our society.

Ayah No.	Theme	Heart Therapy Du'a
1 to 5	Manners of meeting and greeting the Messenger • Respect Authority • Watch Your Tongue • Respect Privacy	Ibn Abbas reported: The Prophet, peace and blessings be upon him, said: رَبِّ اجْعَلْنِي لَكَ شَكَّارًا لَكَ ذَكَّارًا لَكَ رَهَّابًا لَكَ مِطْوَاعًا لَكَ مُخْبِتًا إِلَيْكَ أَوَّاهًا مُنِيبًا رَبِّ تَقَبَّلْ تَوْبَتِي وَاغْسِلْ حَوْبَتِي وَأَجِبْ دَعْوَتِي وَثَبِّتْ حُجَّتِي وَسَدِّدْ لِسَانِي وَاهْدِ قَلْبِي وَاسْلُلْ سَخِيمَةَ صَدْرِي O Lord, make me grateful to you, mindful of you, fearful of you, obedient to you, humble to you, turning to you and repenting. O Lord, accept my repentance, wash away my sin, answer my supplication, establish my proof, direct my tongue, guide my heart, and remove the hatred from my chest. *Source: https://sunnah.com/tirmidhi:3551*

6 to 8	When you hear news, check the facts.	Shakal ibn Humayd said, "Messenger of Allah, teach me a supplication that will benefit me." He said, "Say اللَّهُمَّ عَافِنِي مِنْ شَرِّ سَمْعِي، وَبَصَرِي، وَلِسَانِي، وَقَلْبِي، وَشَرِّ مَنِيِّي O Allah, indeed I seek refuge in You from the evil of my hearing and the evil of my sight, and the evil of my tongue and the evil of my heart, and the evil of my semen. *Source: https://sunnah.com/tirmidhi:3492*
9 to 10	Standing up for justice and creating peace	Narrated Abu Hurairah: The Messenger of Allah (ﷺ) used to say: اللَّهُمَّ إِنِّي أَعُوذُ بِكَ مِنْ قَلْبٍ لاَ يَخْشَعُ وَدُعَاءٍ لاَ يُسْمَعُ وَمِنْ نَفْسٍ لاَ تَشْبَعُ وَمِنْ عِلْمٍ لاَ يَنْفَعُ أَعُوذُ بِكَ مِنْ هَؤُلاَءِ الأَرْبَعِ "O Allah, I seek refuge in You from four things: Knowledge which does not profit, a heart which is not submissive, a soul which has an insatiable appetite, and a supplication which is not heard." *Source: https://sunnah.com/abudawud:1548*
11	Behaviours that lead to conflict	Zayd ibn Arqam reported: The Messenger of Allah, peace and blessings be upon him, said: اللَّهُمَّ آتِ نَفْسِي تَقْوَاهَا وَزَكِّهَا أَنْتَ خَيْرُ مَنْ زَكَّاهَا O Allah, grant my soul a sense of righteousness and purify it, for you are the best purifier. *Source: https://sunnah.com/muslim:2722*
12	Suspicions undermine relationships	Umar bin Al-Khattab said: "The Messenger of Allah taught me, 'Say: اللَّهُمَّ اجْعَلْ سَرِيرَتِي خَيْرًا مِنْ عَلاَنِيَتِي وَاجْعَلْ عَلاَنِيَتِي صَالِحَةً O Allah, make my secret better than my apparent condition, and make my apparent condition righteous. *Source: https://sunnah.com/tirmidhi:3586*

| 13 | Our common humanity | 'Abdullah bin Mas'ud (May Allah be pleased with him) reported:

The Prophet (ﷺ) used to supplicate:

اللَّهُمَّ إِنِّي أَسْأَلُكَ الهُدَى ، والتُّقَى ، والعَفَافَ ، والغِنَى

O Allah! I beseech You for guidance, piety, chastity and contentment. [Muslim].
Source: https://sunnah.com/muslim:2721a |
| 14 to 18 | The true nature of faith | Du'a from the Quran, Surah Al-A'raf: 126

رَبَّنَا أَفْرِغْ عَلَيْنَا صَبْرًا وَتَوَفَّنَا مُسْلِمِينَ

Our Lord! Shower us with perseverance, and let us die while submitting to You |

WORLD #QURANHOUR 2018:
AL-HUJURAT CALL TO ACTION

An Outline to Ummah Ethical Conduct

(QS Al Hujurat, 49: 1-18)

"The believers are nothing else than brothers (in Islamic religion). So make reconciliation between you brothers, and fear Allah, that you may receive mercy."
QS Al-Hujurat, 10

Display respect in behaviour and language while addressing Rasulullah SAW (49:1-5)

Verification of reports (49:6-8)

To establish peace among members of Community (49:9)

Upholding Muslim Brotherhood (49:10)

Condemnation of revealing, defaming and being sarcastic to people (49:11)

Gravity of Suspicion, Spying and backbiting (49:12)

The value of Taqwa (49:13)

Sincerity of Iman and its impact (49:14-18)

UMMAHIKHLAS

APPENDICES

Additional Reflection Questions

1. What do you understand by the first prohibition stated in this surah?

2. Look at the second call to all believers - the 2nd prohibition. How can we apply "lowering our voice to the Prophet" when he is no longer with us?

3. Respecting people's privacy is a command that is nowadays neglected. Do you agree?

4. How can having patience help us in upholding this ethical value?

5. Who are the Saadiqoon mentioned in this surah?

6. Can you summarize the commands and prohibitions pertaining to social conduct and ethics relayed by this surah?

7. What illnesses do you see to be rooted in the current state of ummah? How severe are they?

8. Look around you. The society you live in. Those closest to you. How aware are they about the challenges faced by the Muslims around the world?

9. Is kindness to be shown to all mankind or just the Muslims?

10. How to truly love our brothers and sisters in Islam such that we want more good for them than for us?

11. Are you troubled by how the Muslim youth progress in this era of digital technology and borderless world? What can we do to help the youth and future generation get closer to the Qur'an?

12. Gender equality. What are your thoughts on them?

13. How to eradicate the "I am better than you" mind set?

14. Do you think corruption in our society stems from ill-thoughts or selfishness?

15. Do we investigate just the bad news that we receive or all news?

16. Are we not allowed to make an assumption in dealing with people? Isn't assumption a form of precaution?

Additional Reflection Tips

There are many ways to do a reflection. Here are some additional tips for us to start with this noble act of worship.

1. Reflect on the wonders of Allah's dazzling creation, the inward and outward signs of His Ability and the signs He has scattered abroad the realm of the earth and the heavens. This kind of reflection will increase your knowledge of the Essences, Attributes and Names of Allah.

2. Reflect on the wondrous creatures Allah has made and on yourself. For example, Allah has said, *"On earth there are signs for those with sure faith, and in yourselves too, do you not see?"* (59:20-21). So look at yourself and reflect on the wonders of your own creation.

3. Reflect on the favours of Allah and His bounties which He has caused to reach you. This kind of reflection will result in you continuously rendering thanks to Allah in a manner that pleases Him. It will also fill your heart with love for Allah.

4. Reflect on Allah's complete awareness of you and His seeing and knowing all about you. This will result in you feeling ashamed before Allah should He see you where He has forbidden you to be or miss you where He has commanded you to be.

5. Reflect on your shortcomings in worshipping Allah, and your exposing yourself to His wrath should you do what He has forbidden you. This kind of reflection will increase your consciousness of Allah, encourage you to blame and reproach yourself so that you persevere.

6. Reflect on this worldly life, its numerous preoccupations, hazards and the swiftness with which it perishes and upon the Hereafter and its felicity and permanence. This will result in losing all desire for the world and in wishing for the Hereafter.

7. Reflect on the imminence of death and the regret and remorse which occur when it is too late. The benefit of this kind of reflection is that hopes become short, better behaviour and provision is gathered for the Appointed Day.

8. Reflect on those attributes and acts by which Allah has described His friends and His enemies, and on the immediate and delayed rewards which He has prepared for each group. The benefit of this kind of reflection is that you come to love the fortunate, habituate yourself to emulating their behaviour and taking on their qualities, and detest the wretched and habituate yourself to avoiding their behaviour and traits of character.

These reflection tips are adopted from The Book of Assistance by Imam 'Abdallah Ibn 'Alawi Al-Haddad.

Learning Resources & References

There are numerous Qur'an learning resources and reading materials available. We recommend the following to be used together with this workbook.

The links for all resources listed here (and more) can be retrieved from this link https://bit.ly/QWBresources or via this QR code.

Quran Translation, Tadabbur & Tafsir

1. **12 Keys to Enrich Your Engagement with the Qur'an** by Shaykh Sohaib Saeed

2. **Keys to Tadabbur: How To Reflect Deeply on the Qur'an** article on Yaqeen Institute website

3. **Qur'an for All** app and website by Al Huda International for brief and detailed explanation of this surah and the whole Qur'an

4. **Bayyinah TV** website and app by Bayyinah Institute

5. **Journey Through The Quran: An overview of all 114 chapters** book by Sharif Hasan Al-Banna

6. **The Majestic Quran: A summary of the 30 chapters** by Dr Musharraf Hussain

7. **A Tentative Guide to the Themes of the Surahs of the Qur'an book** by H.R.H. Prince Ghazi bin Muhammad

8. **The Clear Quran and Dictionary** by Dr Mustafa Khattab

9. **Quran.com** website that offers multiple translations and links to other Qur'an learning websites, especially to **QuranReflect** where scholars and learners of Qur'an share their daily Qur'an Tadabbur.

10. **QuranHive** website and mobile app by a small group of Quran enthusiasts seeking to create a platform that facilitates a deeper learning experience of the Quran.

11. **The Quranic Arabic Corpus** website for those studying Qur'anic Arabic

Surah Al-Hujurat

1. **Behind The Apartments** book by Shaykh Ahmed Hammuda

2. **Tafseer Soorah Al-Hujurat** book by Abu Ameenah Bilal Philips

3. **Tafsir Surah Al-Hujurat** by Tuan Guru Dato' Seri Hj. Hadi Abdul Awang (in Bahasa Malaysia)

Allah's Names & Attributes

1. Ramadan 2016 Beautiful Names of Allah by Shaykh Yasir Qadhi

2. Lecture by Taimiyyah Zubair, 2020

3. **Reflecting on the Names of Allah** book, Al Buruj Press 2020 by Jinan Yousef

4. Al Maghrib online course: **The Majesty**

Bibliography

1. **The Majestic Qur'an: A Plain English Translation** by Dr Musharraf Hussain (Paperback First Edition April 2020)

2. **The Most Excellent Names of Allah** by Abu Ahmed Farid

3. **The Book of Assistance** by Imam 'Abdallah Ibn 'Alawi Al-Haddad

Learning Source Tracker

No.	Date Referred	Learning Source Details